CONTENTS

Some words are shown in bold, **like this**. You can find out what they mean by looking in the glossary.

INTRODUCTION: WHAT'S THE DIFFERENCE BETWEEN SEARCH AND RESEARCH?

Computer search and research are two different things. Computer search is the first step, when you use a computer to find information. Research is the second step: looking at the information carefully, to decide whether it is useful.

Computer trick or treat

One way of understanding the difference between search and research is to compare it to trick or treating. First, you go out and gather as many sweets and treats as possible. This is like the "search" phase.

▲Before getting a puppy, you need to find out how to care for it. The Internet would be one good place to search.

Once the treat-gathering phase is finished, you can examine the spoils. In one pile you put the things you want to keep. In another pile are the items that are no good to you. This is like the research phase: deciding which information to keep, and which to abandon.

THE KNOWLEDGE

The first-ever tool for searching the internet was invented in 1990. It was called Archie – *archive* without the *v*. The first proper search engine was probably W3Catalog, which appeared in 1993.

Paul Mason

raintree
...ildren

Raintree is an imprint of Capstone Global Library Limited, a company incorporated in England and Wales having its registered office at 7 Pilgrim Street, London, EC4V 6LB – Registered company number: 6695582

www.raintreepublishers.co.uk
myorders@raintreepublishers.co.uk

Edited by Linda Staniford and Chris Harbo
Designed by Richard Parker and Tim Bond
Original illustrations © Capstone Global Library 2015
Illustrated by Nigel Dobbyn (Beehive Illustration)
Picture research by Jo Miller
Production by Victoria Fitzgerald
Originated by Capstone Global Library Ltd
Printed and bound in China by CTPS

ISBN 978 1 406 28976 3 (hardback)
18 17 16 15 14
10 9 8 7 6 5 4 3 2 1

ISBN 978 1 406 28981 7 (paperback)
19 18 17 16
10 9 8 7 6 5 4 3 2 1

British Library Cataloguing in Publication Data
A full catalogue record for this book is available from the British Library.

Acknowledgements
We would like to thank the following for permission to reproduce photographs:

Alamy: Business/Stephen Barnes, 19 bottom right, © ianmurray, 38, SCPhotos, 31 bottom right, © Sami Sarkis RLD, 13, © wonderlandstock, 7; Getty Images: Hulton Archive / Stringer, 29, Getty Images Sport/ Jeff Kardas, 12, Dorling Kindersley/Steve Lyne, 17; iStockphoto: ©airn, 32 bottom, © ac_bnphotos, 27 inset, ©bogdansemenescu, 4, ©4kodiak, 27, Shutterstock: Blend Images, 24, Jaromir Chalabala, 15(dog), gillmar15 (cat), Glovatskiy, 20, Kamira, 40, Viktoria Kazakova, cover, kellyreekolibry, 31 top left, Dan Kosmayer, 36, mikeledray, 22, Monkey Business Images, 34, 41, michaeljung, 43, Sergey Novikov, 19 top left, DavidPinoPhotography, 32 top, Schubbel, 15, Jaren Jai Wicklund, 35.

Design Elements: Shutterstock: HunThomas, vectorlib.com (throughout) Jaren Jai Wicklund

We would like to thank Andrew Connell for his invaluable help in the preparation of this book.

Every effort has been made to contact copyright holders of material reproduced in this book. Any omissions will be rectified in subsequent printings if notice is given to the publisher.

Searching and the internet

It is possible to search for information on your own computer's **hard drive**, for example by looking at an encyclopaedia that has been stored there. However, almost all computer searching and researching is done on the internet, using a **search engine**.

Fox Terriers - Image Results

More **Fox Terriers** images

Fox Terrier - Wikipedia, the free encyclopedia
en.wikipedia.org/wiki/Fox_terrier   Cached
History | Modern breeds | Common health issues | References
Fox Terriers are two different breeds of the **terrier** dog type: the Smooth **Fox Terrier** and the Wire **Fox Terrier**. Both of these breeds originated in the 19th century ...

Smooth **Fox Terrier** Information and Pictures, Smooth **Fox** ...
www.dogbreedinfo.com/smoothfoxterrier.htm   Cached
All about the Smooth **Fox Terrier**, info, pictures, rescues, care, temperament, health, puppies and much more

◀This shows the first three web pages from a total of over two million found by an Internet search engine. They *all* contain information about fox terrier puppies. Deciding which ones are the most useful will require some research

TECHNICALLY SPEAKING

For understanding the internet and how it works, the technical knowledge in these panels will be useful. For example, you might want to know how to keep **spiders** out of your computer – but these are not creepy crawlies! Turn to page 10 to find out the truth.

What is the internet?

The internet is a network of computers that covers most of the world. It is made up of lots of different kinds of computer, plus the connections between them. Many computers connect to the internet using the phone system.

The network allows computers to send information to and fro. It is like a huge, incredibly high-speed postal service. But it sends **virtual** communications from one computer to another, rather than sending actual letters and packages.

True and false on the internet

The internet is not like school, where a teacher gives you a lower grade if what you have written is not correct. On the internet, there are no grades that tell you whether something you read is true or false. Even websites that look professional may contain false information. Only research can tell computer users whether the information they find on the internet is correct.

laptop

INTERNET

router

◄Information flows from the internet to computers. It can also flow in the opposite direction, from a computer on to the internet.

desktop computer

tablet

wireless connection

wired connection

▲The internet has lots of sources of information, including many different kinds of text, videos, photos and artwork.

THE KNOWLEDGE

Almost any computer can be used for searching and researching. It is usually easiest on a computer with a fairly big screen, as this makes information easier to read. Best are probably:

- Desktop computers
- Laptop computers
- Tablets and mini tablets/notebooks

Internet searches can also be done on E-readers, smartphones, and some games consoles.

TECHNICALLY SPEAKING

The internet is a global network of computers. The web (sometimes called the World Wide Web) is made up of information contained on the internet.

CHAPTER 1: HOW DOES A COMPUTER SEARCH WORK?

Computers search the internet by using a search engine. There are lots of different search engines. There are important differences between them (see pages 18 and 19 to find out more), but most work in a similar basic way.

Collecting information

Search engines find and organise information from the internet. First, they trawl the internet, looking on websites for particular words. For example, the search engine might look on websites for "puppies" or "basketball".

Next, the search engine makes a list, or **index**, of the sites that use the words it has searched for. Under "puppies" it would list sites that mentioned that word. A site that uses the word a lot gets a higher place in the index than one that only uses it a few times.

Search Engine Market Share, February 2012

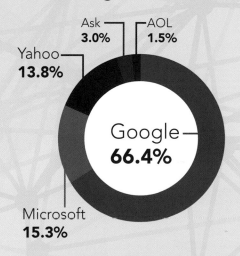

Ask
3.0%

AOL
1.5%

Yahoo
13.8%

Google
66.4%

Microsoft
15.3%

▲In 2012, Google was the most-used search engine by far. A good researcher uses a variety of search engines, not only one.

THE KNOWLEDGE

Today's most popular search engines have indexed hundreds of millions of internet entries. They handle tens of millions of searches every 24 hours. Search engines never sleep. They add hundreds of web pages to their indexes every second.

Pointing searchers to the right place

When someone begins a computer search, the search engine checks its index. Where on the internet can the searcher find information about puppies, for example? The engine lists the pages it has found that mention them, in page after page of results.

One important thing to remember about search engines is that they do not search the whole internet every time you do a search. They search their own index of the internet.

Try this!

Ask an adult to help you do two internet searches for "fox terrier puppy care". Use Google for one search and DuckDuckGo for the other. The results will be different. This tells you that the two search engines have different indexes.

Spider indexes

Search engines build up their indexes using spiders! These spiders don't have long legs, or scare people who are frightened of our eight-legged friends. They are actually **software robots**. They crawl around on the web, looking for whatever the search engine has told them to look for.

The spider begins its journey at a popular website or **server**. It records the words it finds there (though usually it misses out common words such as *the* and *a*). The spider also often notices where on the page words are found. Words in a heading, for example, are more likely to be important.

Having indexed one site, the spider then follows any **links** to other sites. The spider indexes these new sites, then follows *their* links to still more sites. A group of spiders can index hundreds of web pages per second, so they can quickly build up an enormous index.

Web spider

'Crawls' pages

Science
Cars
Travel
Comics
Cinema
Insects
Animals

Builds index

Builds word list

Stores data

Encodes data

Website designers often add links (the full name for these is **hyperlinks**) to the site. These are words or images that, when you click on them, take you to other websites or other parts of the site you are on. The link leads you to more information, an explanation or a new subject that is connected to the one you are reading about.

hyperlink

hyperlink

TECHNICALLY SPEAKING

Not all search engines take the same approach to indexing:

- At one extreme, they may index every word
- At the other extreme, a search engine may index only headings, subheadings, **meta tags** (see page 12), and the most frequently used words.

Most search engines fall somewhere between the two extremes.

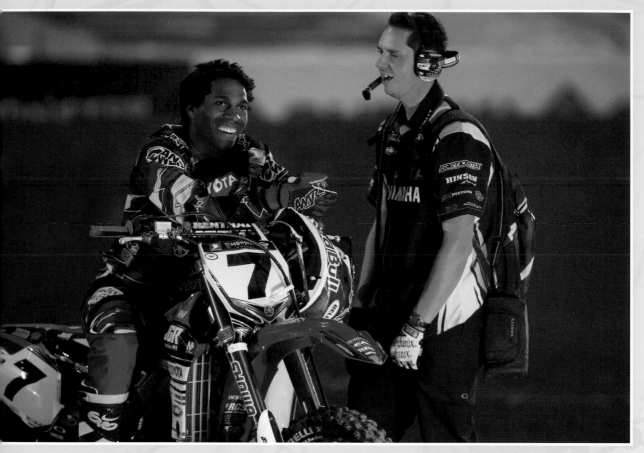

▲US supercross charger Bubba Stewart. He has lots of fans - but what are the best places to find Bubba on the internet? Hopefully, meta tags will help!

Meta tags

Meta tags are a way of making spiders take special notice of something on a web page. The person who creates the web page sets up the tags. They are like hanging up a signpost for the spiders, saying, "Get your information here!"

The owner of a fan site for the American supercross star Bubba Stewart, for example, might add meta tags for "Bubba Stewart", "supercross", "SX", "fan", "African-American" and "racer". When an indexing spider crawls through the site, it will know these words were especially important. People doing a search for "African-American supercross racer" will be more likely to be directed to the site.

Cheeky taggers!

Some website owners try to attract visitors to their site by adding meta tags for popular subjects (for example, "World Series tickets", "One Direction" or "Leonardo di Caprio"). The trouble is, the sites do not actually have any information about these subjects! Thankfully, indexing spiders are too smart to be fooled. They compare the meta tags with the words that actually appear on the site. If the two don't agree, the spiders ignore the meta tag.

TECHNICALLY SPEAKING

There are a *lot* of indexing spiders crawling around the internet. Some sites, for example gaming sites, change all the time. Having spiders crawling through them recording changes would slow the game play down. So the site owners set a robot exclusion protocol, which stops the spiders from crawling through their web pages.

▲Without the robot exclusion protocol, the internet games played on computers would probably work noticeably more slowly.

Boolean operators

Boolean operators are words such as *and, or, not, followed by* and *near*. They are part of the language of internet searches. Using these words is a good way to get exactly the search results you want. The most common are shown on these pages:

and

Putting *and* between words means that only pages that contain all the words will appear in search results. (The search engine will not look for *and*, just the other words.) Some search engines use + instead of *and*.

or

Putting *or* between two (or more) words will mean that at least one of the words must feature on a website for it to be included in the search results.

not

This is a way of making sure things do not appear in your search results. You might, for instance, search for "Manchester and City not United", to prevent Manchester United sites appearing.

followed by

Only websites where the words appear in exactly the order you have given will be listed. For example, "New Forest followed by horse riding" would produce only websites featuring New Forest horse riding.

near

This is short for *within 10 words*. So searching for "California near surfing" will produce a list of websites where the words *California* and *surfing* appear no more than 10 words from one another.

AND

= only material featuring a dog AND a cat

 OR

= material featuring a dog OR a cat

 NOT

= featuring a dog, but NOT a cat

▲Using the right Boolean operators will help you get the exact results you want.

Try this!

To see how Boolean operators can affect a search, try this:

1. Search for "fox and terrier and puppy and care"

2. Open a new window, but use the same search engine to search for "fox terrier puppy care"

3. Compare the two windows. The results will be different: the Boolean operators have affected them.

CHAPTER 2: WHAT MAKES AN EFFECTIVE SEARCH?

Computers cannot read anyone's mind. They can only do what people ask them to do. So, putting a vague subject into a search engine will produce vague results. Using carefully chosen search terms will produce more useful results.

General search terms

General search terms can be useful at the beginning of a search. The results provide background information, plus ideas for new search terms.

At this stage, it is important not to let search terms be affected by what you already know. For example, imagine someone writing a report on famous England footballers. A David Beckham fan might be tempted to search for "David Beckham". But a search for "top ten English footballers" would give much wider results.

THE KNOWLEDGE

The following are signs that a website is likely to contain reliable information.

- Sites with addresses ending in .org, .edu and .gov, which are often run by government or educational organizations.
- A well written, clear site, with no grammatical and spelling mistakes.
- Clear author qualifications (this includes whether the site is from a credible body, such as a famous museum).
- Detailed information, with facts rather than opinions.
- Sites that are not trying to sell something (a product or an idea).

TECHNICALLY SPEAKING

Some website owners use **SEO** (Search Engine Optimisation), a way of moving a site further up a search engine's results list. SEO means that the first site you see on the list of results may not be the most useful or relevant.

Specific search terms

After a general search, the search terms can be made more specific. The football report writer, for example, might have found three or four people who appear in every top ten list. Searching for each one by name will give more detailed information about them.

1) You just got a fox terrier puppy, and you need to find information about him on the internet:

fox terrier puppy

2) The first thing you want to know is whether the puppy needs grooming:

fox terrier + grooming

3) There are two types of fox terriers, with different types of hair!

wire haired fox terrier + grooming

4) You discover your puppy needs a special comb, called a puppy comb, until he is older:

wire haired fox terrier + puppy comb

Using a variety of search engines

To get the widest range of search results, experienced researchers use more than one search engine. They do this because not all search engines are the same. For example:

• Some search engines specialise in particular types of information. Someone who wants to find out a computer-game cheat, for example, might get good results from a search engine that specialises in the subject.

• Other search engines index only particular areas of the internet, or unusual types of pages, such as whole book texts or quotations.

• There are even search engines that collect together the results from other search engines.

Specialist engines often produce different results from a general search engine.

Try this!

Use your favourite search engine to look up "tsunami". Now open two new windows and use the same search term in mahalo.com and yippy.com. The results will be different. Which do you think would be most useful for writing a report?

▲Which place are you most likely to be able to find specialist information? Somewhere that specialises, of course!

THE KNOWLEDGE

There are thousands of search engines on the internet. These are just a few that work in different ways:

- ask.com: a natural-language search engine, which lets you ask a question as if you were asking a teacher or friend

- yippy.com: a "Deep Web" search engine, which indexes pages most indexing spiders do not reach

- mahalo.com: one of several human-powered engines, mahalo's index is reviewed by humans before **content** is included

- duckduckgo.com: this engine suggests ways to narrow down the information (called disambiguation)

▲Organising the results of your computer research makes it much easier to find the information you need at any given moment. Otherwise, each time you want to remind yourself of something, you will probably end up looking through your entire set of results.

THE KNOWLEDGE

One way to save results from an internet search is to cut and paste interesting information into a new document. The trouble with cut and paste, though, is that it is easy to forget where the information came from. Some people even get confused and think someone else's work is their own. To avoid this, always make a note of where information has come from.

TECHNICALLY SPEAKING

Screen grabs (sometimes called screen shots) are snapshots of an area of a computer screen. They can be used to record sample results. Including web addresses in screen grabs makes it easy to go back to the same site later.

Organising results

Good researchers organise their search results. It makes it easier to find specific bits of information later. There are several ways to do this:

1. Print out

The printouts can be organised into folders (or just piles). A good way to start is with file names using your original specific search terms. For the project on pages 16 and 17, there could be a folder called "top tens" and other folders for each famous footballer.

2. Save on the computer

It's also possible to save search results onto the computer. Like the piles of paper, the results can be organised using folders and **sub-folders** on your computer's hard drive.

3. Save web addresses

Search results can be saved in the form of web addresses, which you can go back to later. It is important to keep a note of what information the website holds. For example, an article on tsunamis might have websites listed under headings such as "recent examples", "history" and "causes". Each website listed would also need a short description, such as, "Boxing Day 2004 tsunami in Java".

p.16
[A]
WHAT MAKES AN EFFECTIVE SEARCH?
https://blogs.glowscotland.org.uk/fa/ICTFalkirkPrimaries/tag/google/
http://primarytech.global2.vic.edu.au/2012/05/29/tentips-for-teaching-students-how-to-research-and-filter-information/

[Intro]
Computers cannot read anyone's mind. They can only do what people ask them to do. So, putting a vague subject into a search engine will produce vague results. Using carefully chosen search terms will produce more-useful results.
37

[B]
1) General search terms
General search terms can be useful at the beginning of a search. The results provide background information, plus ideas for new search terms.

At this stage, it is important not to let search terms be affected by what you already know. For example, imagine someone writing a report on famous England footballers. A David Beckham fan might be tempted to search for "David Beckham". But a search for "top ten English footballers" would give much wider results.
78

[B]
2) Specific search terms
After a general search, the search terms can be made more specific. The football report writer, for example, might have found three or four people who appear in every top ten list. Searching for each one by name will give more detailed information about them.
45

▲Unless you take notes about where information has come from, and organize your work carefully, you could end up accidentally using someone else's work as your own. This is called plagiarism (see page 36) and is not allowed.

CHAPTER 3: HOW DO YOU TURN SEARCH INTO RESEARCH?

A researcher is like a trick-or-treater who's collected a big bag of sweets. The bag might contain some revolting lavender drops – yeuw! These need to be identified and dumped, so that only the top-quality sweets remain.

Sorting information

Information you have searched for and gathered from the internet is like a trick-or-treater's sweets – a mixed bag. Some will probably be incorrect. This incorrect information is the lavender drops. It needs to be identified and dumped.

▲A good researcher acts like a detective at a crime scene. Detectives start by finding out everything about the crime. Then they examine the evidence, to decide which pieces are important and which can be ignored.

TECHNICALLY SPEAKING

Crowdsourcing is a name for getting information about a subject from lots of different people. They can all review and change the piece of work (for example, an article about tsunamis). Online sites such as Wikipedia use crowdsourcing to produce their content.

Care is needed during this process, though – it is easy to feel that something that does not agree with what you already think must be unreliable or inaccurate. This is not necessarily so. When evaluating information, researchers are careful not to let what they think they know affect their results. Instead, they check facts that seem incorrect or surprising, to see whether they are true or not.

THE KNOWLEDGE

Researchers always note the date when something was written. Dates can be important. For example, if you are looking up the world record for the highest BMX jump, an article from 2005 might not be accurate. The record could easily have been broken since then.

► When doing research using a computer, remember that not everything you read will be 100% reliable. Lots of people who put material on the internet like to make their opinions sound like facts!

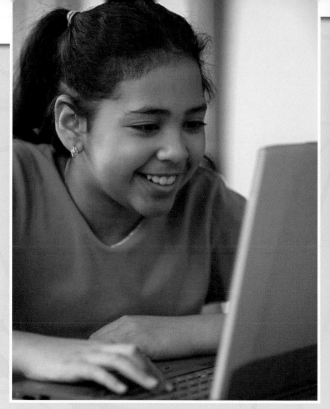

Types of information

There are all kinds of websites on the internet. When researching something, it is important to be able to tell one from another. Key types of websites that appear in search results include:

Content/information sites

Websites such as Wikipedia, About.com, and the websites of museums and government departments.

Good things: Often give a clear summary of the subject.

Possible problems: Crowdsourced sites are unlikely to be 100% correct, because mistakes are only corrected if someone notices them.

Blogs and microblogs

Blogs and **microblogs** such as blogger, wordpress, and tumblr.

Good things: A good way to look at lots of different opinions quickly.

Possible problems: Bloggers sometimes make their opinion look like fact, which can lead to confusion. It is unlikely anyone has checked the writer's work is correct.

Community sites/chatrooms/forums

These are usually about specific interests (for example BMX racing, surf-mat riding or being in a choir).

Good things: Can be a good **source** of expert advice, and a wide range of opinions.

Possible problems: Hard to be sure whether the people giving advice are qualified, and some writers think their own opinions are facts.

Question-and-answer sites

Sites where people can send in questions to see if anyone watching knows the answer.

Good things: A good way to get a variety of answers quickly.

Possible problems: These sites often give you a "best answer", but it is impossible to know whether the answer is actually correct.

◄Correcting every error on the internet would take a very, very long time.

The CARS checklist

The CARS checklist is a good way to work out whether a website is likely to be a good source of useful information. CARS stands for Credibility, Accuracy, Reasonableness and Support.

CARS 1: Credibility

Credibility is another word for believability. When researchers look at information they ask themselves: Should we believe this?

For a website to be believable, the author (who can be an individual writer or an organisation) should have experience or education relevant to the subject. Anyone can write an article about tsunami risks, for example. But someone who works for the emergency services, or a government agency, is more likely to know about the subject.

THE KNOWLEDGE

These warning signs suggest that a text is not credible:

1. It is not clear who the author is.
2. There is bad grammar, and/or a lot of spelling mistakes.
3. Lots of negative comments appear in the Comments section.
4. The author uses emotional language, for example: "The evil victors murdered thousands of their prisoners in cold blood."

C.A.R.S. **CREDIBILITY** Is the source of the information qualified?

CARS 2: Accuracy

Accuracy simply means correctness. First, find out when something was written, and whether this could have an effect on its accuracy. Even something from a credible source written years ago may not still be accurate today.

Accuracy can also be affected by who an article is aimed at. An article about how engines work that a 9-year-old could understand would not have enough information for a motor engineer.

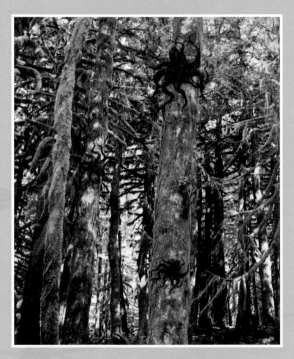

▲The Pacific Tree Octopus appears on a very convincing website – even though there is no such thing as a Pacific Tree Octopus!

THE KNOWLEDGE

These warning signs suggest that a text may be inaccurate:

- There is no date, so it is not clear when the text was written.

- An old date on a text about something new or constantly changing.

- There are lots of general statements that cannot always be true, for example: "The Chicago Bears are boring to watch."

ACCURACY
Is the information recent?
Is it detailed enough?

REASONABLENESS
Is the text balanced and fair?

SUPPORT
Are the facts backed up?

27

CARS 3: Reasonableness

What makes a source of information reasonable? These three things are important:

1. Reasonable texts admit that there may be more than one view. For example:

The First World War was caused by German aggression.

vs

Many people think German aggression caused the First World War. Others say that the actions of Russia and France were also responsible.

Which seems more reasonable?

2. Reasonable texts do not **contradict** themselves within the same article. For example:

No one famous has ever come from Lincolnshire.

Then, later in the same article:

The world's most brilliant scientist, Isaac Newton, was born in Lincolnshire.

If the world's greatest scientist came from Lincolnshire, then he is at least one famous person to have come from that county.

3. If the author's opinion becomes clear to the reader, the text may not be reasonable. The author is probably putting a one-sided argument, rather than giving the facts.

For example:

Despite the claims, great white sharks have never been proved to attack humans. As I have repeatedly said, the true culprit is always the bull shark.

C.A.R.S. → CREDIBILITY
Is the source of the information qualified?

THE KNOWLEDGE

These warning signs suggest that a text is not reasonable:

1. The language is emotional or made personal, for example: "The whole DVD is complete rubbish" or "Anyone who disagrees with this is a fool."
2. There are no facts to support what the text says, or opinions have been put forward as facts.
3. The writer gives a one-sided view, without admitting that other views are possible.

THE KNOWLEDGE

Lots of websites claim that the nursery rhyme *Sing a Song of Sixpence* was invented as a secret recruiting rhyme for pirate ships. These websites did not research the story! It is actually a spoof, made up by an **urban-myth** investigation team.

ACCURACY
Is the information recent?
Is it detailed enough?

REASONABLENESS
Is the text balanced and fair?

SUPPORT
Are the facts backed up?

CARS 4: Support

Most information that is available on the internet comes from somewhere else. For example, an article about how to survive a tsunami is not likely to have been written by someone who has survived a tsunami. Instead, the author will probably have gathered information from several different sources.

A good researcher likes to know what sources an author has used, so that he or she can judge whether they are reliable or not. For example:

Climbing a tree is a stupid thing to do during a tsunami.

vs

The Pacific Tsunami Center says that climbing a tree is unlikely to save you during a tsunami.

Finally, if an article makes a surprising claim, the author should provide extra support for it. For example:

Cows are bad for the environment.

vs

Cow burps are causing global warming. The United Nations says that methane – which cows burp out constantly – is one of the most harmful greenhouse gases for the environment.

THE KNOWLEDGE

These warning signs suggest that a text is not well supported:

1. Statistics are given, but without any information about where they came from or when they were produced.
2. The researcher cannot find other sources of information with the same facts. (And even if they can, care is needed: some websites simply cut and paste text from elsewhere. Check that the exact same words have not been used in two sources.)

▲People who can show where their information came from are always easier to believe than those who cannot.

"No - we need to go up a hill!"

"The government says up a HILL is safer!"

CHAPTER 4: HOW DO YOU TURN RESEARCH INTO RESULTS?

Once you have researched a subject, you will have a lot of good-quality information. You will probably be keen to start writing! This chapter shows some of the things good writers do to turn their research into results.

Reorganising research results

Imagine someone trying to write a 750-word report for people going on holiday in a tsunami zone. Their research has given them a good idea of what information is available. Armed with this, the writer can start sketching out a basic plan for the report. He or she might decide to have five 150-word sections called:

1. What is a tsunami?

2. Are all tsunamis dangerous?

3. What are the warnings a tsunami is coming?

4. Can you prepare for a tsunami?

5. How do you survive a tsunami?

These headings can be used to organise the research. For example, "What is a tsunami?" would have the information on what causes tsunami, how often they happen, and how big they are. When the writer comes to write that section, all the research will be gathered together ready.

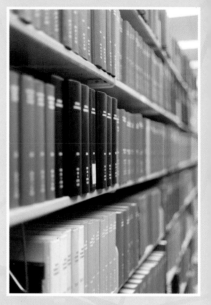

Which is easier to use – organised or disorganised information?

▲Organising your information into folders and sub-folders, like these, is a good way to start turning your research into results.

▶Alternatively, you could organise your results in a single document, like this.

TSUNAMI REPORT

What is a tsunami?
From Australian Beachsafe organisation:
http://beachsafe.org.au/tsunami/ema/pag-es/04

Are all tsunamis dangerous?
News reports on 2013 tsunami in Solomon Islands
www.usatoday.com/story/news/world/2013/02/07/solomon-islands-tsuna-mi/1897891
www.cnn.com/2013/02/05/world/asia/solo-mon-islands-quake

News summary of Boxing Day 2004 tsunami:
http://news.bbc.co.uk/onthisday/hi/dates/sto-ries

THE KNOWLEDGE

Research throws up lots of different types of information, including photos, diagrams, and quotes. There are two ways to organise these:

1. All together in one sub-folder – this is best if there are only a few.
2. Separately, with the relevant sections (for example, "What is a tsunami?"). This is best if there are a lot.

▲If you want to publish work on a blog, ask an adult to help you set it up.

Starting to write

To start writing a section – for example, "What is a tsunami?" – the writer opens that folder. Inside will be all the research results for this section. Rereading these before writing reminds the writer of anything he or she has forgotten.

Sub-sections

Before writing each section, it can be helpful to divide it into sub-sections. "What is a tsunami?", for example, could be divided into "Causes", "Frequency" and "Size". If the whole section is to be 150 words long, each sub-section will need to be about 50 words long.

Where to begin?

Most writers prefer to begin by writing the first section, then the second, and so on. However, as long as the research has been divided into sections, it should be possible to write them in any order.

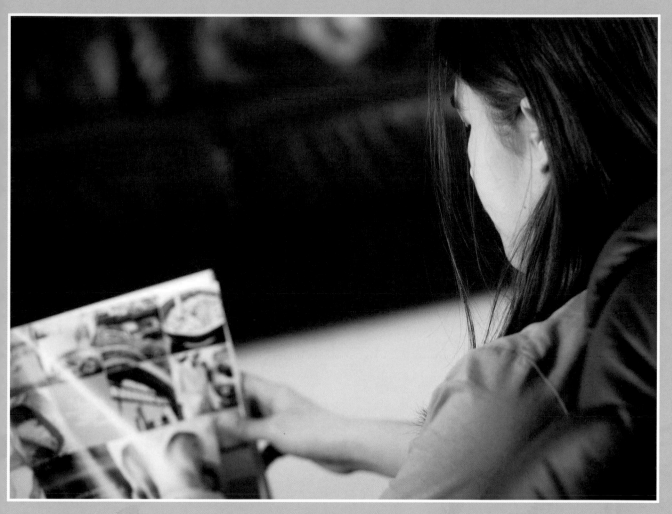

▲Adding images to a piece of work often makes it more interesting to read, and easier to remember as well.

THE KNOWLEDGE

Photos and artwork can add a lot to a piece of written work. For example, saying that some tsunamis are as tall as a three-storey house becomes more real next to a photo of someone standing next to a three-storey house! To work well, images should appear close to the words they illustrate.

Respecting other people's work

When turning research into results, it is important to respect other people's work. For example, writers must never pretend other people's work is their own, or use someone else's work without permission.

Watch out – plagiarism about!

Plagiarism is copying someone else's work and pretending it is your own. Writers are allowed to include other people's words and ideas in their work, but must say where these words and ideas came from. This is called citing or acknowledgement.

▲Cutting and pasting other people's work is fine - as long as you do not later pretend it is your own. That is called plagiarism and whether done deliberately or by accident it is not allowed.

TECHNICALLY SPEAKING
Checking for plagiarism is very easy:

1. There are several specialist plagiarism checkers on the internet.

2. A quick check is to put suspicious sentences into a search engine, with quotation marks around them. If it has been copied from a website, the results will show where the sentence appears on the internet.

Here are two examples – the first is plagiarism, the second is not:

The Zephyr skate team was all conquering. They were unconventional and they didn't care if they got judged well.

vs

The Zephyr skate team was all conquering. As skating world champion Tom Sims said, "They were unconventional and they didn't care if they got judged well."

Plagiarism is not always this obvious, however. The panel below lists some of the other forms of plagiarism.

THE KNOWLEDGE
This is a selection of plagiarism offences.

1. Copying someone else's work word-for-word.
2. Including big blocks of text that are someone else's words.
3. Using someone else's work but changing a few words so it is not exactly the same.
4. Using someone else's ideas but slightly rewritten.
5. Mixing proper acknowledgement with unacknowledged use of someone else's work.

▲Although a photo search on the internet will call up lots of photographs, none of them are yours. It is important not to act as if they are.

Acknowledgement/citing

If a writer uses someone else's work, adding an acknowledgement means no one can accuse them of plagiarism. The acknowledgement should say:

- The author's name.

- Where the original can be found (for example an internet address or a book title).

- The date it was written.

If someone wants to know more about a particular subject, they can go to the source to find it. And if the source turns out to be wrong, people will be able to see it was not 100% the writer's fault!

Intellectual property

Intellectual property is a way of saying that someone who makes a piece of work owns it. This is common sense – but it can be easy to forget on the internet. Intellectual property includes writing, photos, videos and music. On the internet these are usually free. Just because it is free for everyone to look at, though, does not mean it actually belongs to everyone.

It is easy to drag and drop photos, artwork and other content into a piece of work. It is important not to do this unless you are sure that the owner has given permission.

▲Always respect the © sign – even when it is not actually there!

TECHNICALLY SPEAKING

If something has a © sign next to it, it's a reminder that the person who made the work owns it. Even without the © sign, the maker is still the owner unless they say otherwise.

There's a simple rule for whether or not to use someone else's work: "If in doubt, leave it out."

Fact checking and review

Following the right search and research procedures should mean that the facts in a well-researched piece of work are correct. However, everyone makes mistakes! It is easy to write something down incorrectly or get a number wrong, for example. Good writers always check their own work at least twice:

1. The first check is to make sure the finished piece makes sense and that you have not left out anything you wanted to say. If you are checking a piece of work for school, look back at the original assignment. Have you done what was asked?

2. The second check is to make sure all the facts are correct. Check every fact, paying special attention to any that seem suspicious.

It is also useful for someone else to look at a piece of work before it is finished. They sometimes spot mistakes the author has missed.

▲ As well as checking your own work, it is a great idea to ask someone else to look through it. They can tell you if it makes sense and whether anything could be added or removed.

TECHNICALLY SPEAKING

Peer means a person with similar experience. So, peer review is asking someone like you – someone from school, or the same age – to check your work.
Peer reviewers have to be careful not to let their feelings affect their review. Whether the reviewer likes someone or not, they should give an honest opinion of the work – not the person!

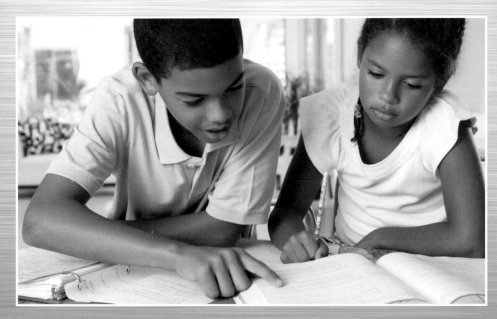

▲ Having someone like you check through your work once it is finished is called peer review.

THE KNOWLEDGE

Put the fact you want to check into a search engine, and make sure that a reliable source (see pages 26–29) confirms the fact is correct.
It is important not to just check the same source again – check the fact is backed up by a different source.

CONCLUSION: TOP 10 TIPS FOR SEARCH AND RESEARCH

The internet contains millions of web pages, which contain all kinds of information. Finding exactly what you want can be like looking for a needle in a haystack. Following our Top Ten Tips will make the job easier and give better results.

1. Remember: there is a difference between search and research. For good results, you need to do both!

SEARCHING

2. When searching for information, use a variety of search engines. They all have different indexes which will produce different results.

3. Use Boolean operators (see pages 14 and 15) to narrow down your search results.

4. Always note where information comes from, so that you can go back and find it again later. (This also stops you forgetting that it is someone else's work.)

RESEARCHING

5. Never think that because something is on a website, or high up in a search results list, it must be correct.

6. Remember there are all kinds of information on the internet. Lots of what you read is opinion, not fact.

7. Use the CARS checklist to decide whether a website is reliable or not.

USING YOUR RESULTS

8. Use the knowledge you have gained through research to make a plan for your work. Use this plan to organise your results.

9. When writing up your results, be careful not to claim other people's work as your own.

10. Always check your work, especially your facts.

◀ Who knows? Maybe if you use a computer really well for researching your schoolwork, it could lead to some prizewinning results.

Try this!

Compare how you would research a subject on the internet now with how you would have done it before reading this book. Make a list of the new things you would do.

GLOSSARY

blog website where a writer can publish their work, usually for free. The things they write appear in time order, with the newest first.

blogging writing a blog

content words, images and design that appear on a website

contradict disagree with

hard drive disc inside a computer where information is stored. Many desktop computers have hard drives. Laptops, tablets and phones often use a different kind of storage, called a "solid state drive" or SSD.

hyperlink word or image that, when you click on it, takes you to a website

index list of items. A search engine's index lists all the information it has found on the internet.

intellectual property ownership of a piece of work. For example, an article about surviving a tsunami is the intellectual property of the person who wrote it.

link another word for hyperlink

meta tag device making search-engine spiders take special notice of something on a website

microblog blog that limits people to a small number of words or a very simple layout. The most popular microblogging sites are twitter and Tumblr.

search engine computer programme that people use to find information on the Internet

SEO short for Search Engine Optimisation, a way of making a website appear higher up in a search engine's results list than it normally would

server super computer designed for a specific task, for example storing information or running a network

software robot piece of computer code that follows instructions given to it by a human programmer

source where information originally came from

spider on the internet, a spider is a software robot that works for a search engine, gathering information for the engine's index

sub-folder folder contained within another folder

urban myth story that is often repeated, but which no one knows is really true or not

virtual created using a computer

FIND OUT MORE

Books

Computer Safety Paul Mason (Raintree, 2014)

Internet Safety Nick Hunter (Raintree, 2011)

Raspberry Pi for Kids Computeractive, Magbook,
 Jonathon Parkyn and Ian Jackson
 (Dennis Publishing, 2013)

A Smart Girl's Guide to the Internet Sharon Miller Cindrich
 (American Girl Publishing, 2009)

Social Networks and Blogs Lori Hile (Raintree Freestyle, 2011)

Internet resources

www.kidrex.org/
This search engine works from an index of pages that have been
created especially for children. It relies on the Google search
engine's SafeSearchTM filters to screen out unsuitable material.

www.kidsclick.org/
Designed especially for young people by librarians. You can
search by subject, media (photos, sound and video) or even
using the Dewey Decimal System that is found in libraries.

http://kidsmart.org.uk/
Kidsmart is a great website for young people to learn about all kinds of computer-based subjects. It includes sections on mobile phones, chatrooms, file sharing, music, games, networking and – most importantly – safe searching on the internet.

http://kidshealth.org/kid/feeling/school/plagiarism.html#
www.plagiarism.org/plagiarism-101/prevention

Each of these websites describes plagiarism and gives useful tips on how to avoid committing it.

www.searchenginewatch.com
This is a good place to start finding out about different search engines. Within the site – at http://tinyurl.com/q5r3fkc – is even a page giving information about some of the search engines you can use to find just the right search engine! This website is designed for use by adults, so you'll need to ask an adult to help you use it.

Places to visit

The National Museum of Computing, Milton Keynes, UK

This museum is at Bletchley Park, where during the Second World War British and the US began to develop the first computers. There are displays and information about these early efforts, as well as later developments in computing.

INDEX